1 The post mill at Great Gransden,
Huntingdonshire. The whole mill was
turned into the wind by means of the
tail pole, the canvas sail cloths being
spread or reefed according to the
strength of the wind. *c.* 1890

Victorian and Edwardian
COUNTRY LIFE
from old photographs

Introduction and commentaries by

JOHN S. CREASEY

B. T. BATSFORD LTD

LONDON

FIRST PUBLISHED 1977
REPRINTED 1983
COPYRIGHT JOHN S. CREASEY 1977

PHOTOTYPESET BY TRADESPOOLS LTD, FROME, SOMERSET
PRINTED IN ENGLAND BY
THE ANCHOR PRESS LTD,
TIPTREE, ESSEX
FOR THE PUBLISHERS B. T. BATSFORD LTD,
4 FITZHARDINGE STREET, LONDON W1H 0AH

ISBN 0 7134 0819 7

2 *Frontispiece* Picking pole-trained hops in east Kent about 1889. The small baskets would be emptied into larger five or six bushel baskets for measuring. Photograph by William Boyer of Sandwich

3 A group of haymakers in Suffolk. The vehicle in front of the stacks is a 'morphey' or hermaphrodite, a cart with an additional forecarriage, which increased its carrying capacity at harvest time. *c.* 1895

Contents

Acknowledgements

Photographic sources: The Author and Publishers wish to thank the following organisations and individuals for allowing copies to be made from original photographs in their possession or for supplying prints:

Abbot Hall Museum of Lakeland Life and Industry, Kendal, 56, 58, 76. Mrs E. Alden, 6. Mr H. Aldridge, 49. The Beaford Centre Photographic Archive, 57, 82, 116. Miss S. Bellamy, 59, 91, 132. Birmingham Public Libraries, 65, 80, 111, 143. Lady C. H. Bonham-Carter, 107. Buckinghamshire County Museum, 13, 30, 60, 87–88, 103, 105, 106. Carlisle Museum and Art Gallery, 33. Country Life, 144. Dorset County Museum, 75, 154. English Folk Dance and Song Society, 148. Miss C. Fisher, 69. Mr R. G. Grace, 25, 102. Mrs A. M. Green, 147. Hampshire County Museum Service, 8, 44–46, 117, 135, 141. Hereford City Library, 19, 92, 101. Hereford and Worcester County Museum, 48, 94. Mr and Mrs Hutchins, 74. Mrs D. N. James, 97. Mrs Luff, 55, 62. Maidstone Museum, 71. Museum of English Rural Life, University of Reading, 4, 9, 10, 11, 12, 14–16, 20–23, 24, 31, 34–35, 38–39, 42–43, 50, 51, 54, 63, 79, 93, 95, 99, 108, 112, 118, 119–120, 125, 129, 133–134, 142, 145. Museum of English Rural Life (Fowler Collection), 28. Museum of English Rural Life (Ransomes Collection), 41. Museum of East Anglian Life, Stowmarket, 124. Museum of Lincolnshire Life, 115. National Union of Agricultural and Allied Workers, 122–123. Mr V. J. Newbury, 64. Norfolk County Library, 26, 152. North of England Open-Air Museum, 17, 32, 61, 77–78, 113, 130, 139, 151. Northumberland County Council, 96. Oxfordshire County Council, Department of Museum Services, 36, 70. Packer's Studio, 37, 52, 150. Pitstone Local History Society, 5, 89, 127–128, 131, 136. Priest's House Museum, Wimborne Minster, 137. Reading Museum and Art Gallery and the Berkshire Archaeological Society, 149. Royal Institution of Cornwall, 53, 126, 153. Salisbury and South Wiltshire Museum, 104. Science Museum by courtesy of Mr E. F. Sidery, 2, 66, 81, 109. Mr F. Smith, 146. Suffolk Record Office, 3, 18, 40, 72, 114, 138, 140. Sutcliffe Gallery, Whitby, 7. Mr C. F. Tebbutt, 98. John Topham Picture Library, 83–86, 121. Mr R. H. Walton, 100. Mr W. G. Waters, 110. Waverley District Museum Service, 27, 29, 47, 67, 73, 90. Plates 1 and 68 are from the Publisher's collection.

The quotation from Frank Sutcliffe is an extract from *Frank Sutcliffe: photographer of Whitby* by Michael Hiley (1974) by permission of Gordon Fraser Gallery, London.

The quotation from Sir Benjamin Stone is an extract from *Customs and faces: photographs by Sir Benjamin Stone, 1838–1914*, by Bill Jay (1972) by permission of Academy Editions, London.

In addition to the individuals and organisations listed in the photographic sources the Author wishes to record his thanks to the following for their assistance in the preparation of this book: Miss R. E. Allen, Mr S. Caunce and Mr J. Gall of the North of England Open-Air Museum; Miss R. J. Ewles, Buckinghamshire County Museum; Mr J. D. Hawkins; Mr S. de Lotbiniere; Mr J. P. Ward, Science Museum; Mr C. Bowden, Waverley District Council.

The Author acknowledges the help and encouragement received from his colleagues at the Museum of English Rural Life. He is particularly indebted to Dr E. J. T. Collins, Mr C. A. Jewell and Dr Sadie B. Ward for their valuable suggestions concerning his text, to Mrs Hilary Woolley who looked at photographs and to two successive secretaries, Mrs Susan Pither and Mrs Jean Sylvester who deciphered his handwriting.

Introduction

The photographs presented here, dating from the 1860s to just before the First World War, portray life and work in the English countryside during a half-century of profound change. To highlight the effect of this change on rural society many of their subjects have been grouped around the two themes of survival of traditional practices and of innovation. The illustrations are selected from the work of photographers who recorded the activities of men and women, their work, home life and relaxation. They are not representative of the many surviving photographs of buildings and landscapes which generally serve less well to document such a period of rapid transition.

In these 50 years Britain's centre of gravity moved decisively to the towns and cities, bringing about a permanent decline in the role played by the countryside in the life of the nation. The changes of the seventeenth and eighteenth centuries within agriculture had helped to bring industrial society into existence. But in the nineteenth century rural England was itself forced to adapt to the needs of the dominant urban society and became transformed by the innovations of industrialism. The full impact of change did not make itself felt until the last quarter of the nineteenth century when British agriculture ceased to be the principal supplier of the nation's food. Then for the first time the demand of the urban population for cheap food coincided with the ability of countries overseas to supply it in bulk and without significant loss of quality. By 1900 most of Britain's wheat, butter, cheese, as well as a large proportion of her meat was imported. Nor was this all, for in the past the countryside had always been a source of other natural products. But from the 1870s the great underwood industry of southern England was slowly declining in importance as its products were replaced by imported timber or metal. Additionally many other small industries, such as brewing, milling and ironfounding, were moved nearer to their markets and sources of raw materials in the larger towns and cities.

On the surface the difference between town and country was becoming more sharply defined. Country towns, like George Sturt's Farnham, in which rural life had grown 'tense and vital' were now losing their close physical relationship with their agricultural hinterland. Yet paradoxically the invisible economic ties binding towns and cities to the rural areas were growing stronger. The countryside around the large conurbations was given over to the specialised production of fruit and vegetables for the city housewife and hay for the large army of city horses. Further afield a marketing revolution had followed the establishment of a national railway network in the 1830s and 1840s which enabled liquid milk to be brought into London from the distant pastures of the north midlands and the south-west. Conversely, the country depended on the towns for a multitude of products from steam engines to tea cups and at busy times for a labour force of city dwellers who poured out from London and the Black Country each autumn to harvest in the hop gardens and orchards of the south-east and of the west midlands.

With the exception of hops all these branches of agriculture, fruit growing, market gardening and pasturing for hay and milk production, increased in size and prosperity as the profitability of corn and sheep farming declined. The Victorian countryside contained many regional differences, for climate, topography and the proximity of markets all influenced the type of agriculture practised and determined the nature of each area's special products and its level of economic well-being. Thus Canon Girdlestone, writing in 1872, found the contrast between the labourer's condition in the north of England and in the west and south-west to be 'almost inconceivable: nothing less than the difference between plenty and starvation, between life and bare existence'.

The introduction of new techniques in agriculture was a very uneven process both between one area of the country and another and within different branches of farming. Hence modern machines and traditional tools coexisted, the flail with the threshing machine, the scythe with the binder, the seed lip with the Suffolk drill. Each had its own special usefulness. There was a period about the turn of the century, when it would have been possible for a traveller through England to have found all of the following types of motive power in regular use: animal draught by both horse and ox; wind and water mills and engines driven by steam, gas, oil and electricity; in addition to the manual labour of men and women. Many farm operations remained to be mechanised by the First World War. Large numbers of workers were still needed to harvest root and potato crops and to pick fruit and hops. The importance of the horse was not affected as there were new tasks after 1840, drawing the mowing and reaping machines, hauling the portable steam engine (unable to move under its own power) and transporting the produce of woods and fields to the railheads. It was the horse that locked together the Victorian transport system, remaining the indispensable means of door-to-door communication for a society continually on the move.

Mobility was a factor of life for those agricultural labourers and small country craftsmen and their families who responded to the lure of higher wages and better conditions. Sons went into factories and the armed forces, daughters into domestic service and whole families migrated to towns or to find new homes overseas. The rural labourers who remained were in one of the worst paid occupations, yet their jobs required long hours, hard physical toil and a high level of skill in the use of tools and machines and the handling of livestock. The farm worker had also to adapt himself to the many different tasks of the agricultural year. He was still in some respects self-reliant, and in certain areas the possession of an allotment and a pig played a vital part in the cottage economy and tipped the balance between mere sufficiency and a small degree of comfort. But essentially the labourer was now a wage earner, dependent on a weekly income to pay the rent and buy food from the shops.

The adaptability of country people was illustrated in the way that so many of them followed multiple occupations, by which they could even out the fluctuations in income caused by the seasonal peaks and troughs of their work. In some villages it was the exception rather than the rule for a man to depend on one source of income alone. Thus a small farmer might also be a carrier or a potter and a woodland worker might become a field labourer for the summer. There were, of course, more specialist workers who followed one calling all their life; men whose occupations developed in them a strong attachment to their native villages and fields. Caleb Bawcombe, the shepherd in W. H. Hudson's *A Shepherd's Life*, felt himself to be in a strange land when he crossed the Wiltshire border to take up employment in Dorset. But the experience of men like George Sturt's Bettesworth was perhaps more typical, for he had travelled widely in his youth and worked in many different places and occupations before returning to the village of his birth. The requirements of the various harvests of the countryside, hay, corn, fruit, hops, underwood, bark and wool created seasonal peaks in demand for labour which, before mechanisation, could only be met by migration of men between one district and another. Thus the labourers around Farnham took in harvests on the Sussex coast before returning home to participate in the local hop picking; Buckinghamshire labourers tramped 'uppards' towards London every year for the hay harvest in Middlesex.

Into the previously self-contained communities came newcomers bringing the values of urban civilisation. These were professional people, including schoolmistresses and the new class of 'villa' dwellers, who lived in the country but worked in the towns, the forerunners of the modern commuter. Richard Jefferies for one believed that the bringing of fashion into the countryside was helping 'that sapping and undermining of the ancient, sturdy simplicity, the solid oak of country character, replacing it with veneer'. To its credit the new industrial state was able to provide some of the means of remedying longstanding deficiencies in the old rural community. Improved standards of hygiene and sanitation, veterinary and medical care, education (the latter hopelessly inadequate for rural needs) and the old age pension, all proved to be of eventual benefit to the still needy villagers of the late nineteenth and early twentieth centuries.

The growing influence of urban culture contributed to the disappearance of those songs, games and customs particularly associated with village life, leaving by the 1880s only what Flora Thompson called their 'last echoes'. There had probably never been a fully developed indigenous folk culture in the English countryside and perhaps Jefferies was correct when he expressed the opinion that 'green meads and rolling lands of wheat . . . have never yet inspired those who dwell upon them with songs, uprising from the soil'. Nevertheless, even if the importance of maypoles, mummers and morris dancing has been exaggerated by the folk revivalists, certainly many of

4 Draught oxen in a farm strawyard in Sussex. *c.* 1885

the traditional forms of rural entertainment were fading out of existence. A feature of the old rural society had been the integration of work and leisure, compartments of life that were to become more rigidly separated in the industrial community. Hence the tension and toil involved in gathering the harvest had been dissipated in the harvest home celebrations and suppers. Labourers and craftsmen had employed their working skills to compete against each other in ploughing matches, hedge-laying and thatching competitions. The hiring fairs, formerly attended by country people, had served both an economic and a recreational purpose. Indeed, the concept of the holiday as a complete break from normal daily work was still alien to the older generation of farmers and labourers at the end of the nineteenth century. One may observe a growing tendency whereby the older more spontaneous forms of recreation were replaced by organised events such as fêtes, concerts and village flower shows. An innovation was the village institute, with its library of improving books and its itinerant lecturers, propagating the values of the more refined levels of society, which flourished under the patronage of rector and squire.

The old rural social order, represented by the gentry and landowning aristocracy, began to break up after the 1870s with the agricultural depression and the declining significance of agriculture within the national economy. The resulting sales of landed estates brought in their place new proprietors who had made their wealth in industry and commerce. In Edwardian England their country houses were filled with guests and field sports flourished as never before.

George Sturt observed that every episode of rural life must have had a beginning as well as an ending and the development of photography ensured the survival of some of these beginnings and endings. The earliest British photographs, taken by Fox Talbot at Lacock Abbey, included rural subjects principally because there they were close at hand. In the 1850s William Grundy took a series of rural views and by the end of the decade unposed subjects were being recorded with the first photographs of urban street scenes. There is, however, a scarcity of rural photographs before 1880, which is not wholly due to the inconvenience of carrying the heavy equipment required for wet plate processing into the countryside.

Such difficulties had not deterred Fenton in the Crimea or Francis Frith in the tough conditions of the Middle East but what interested these two photographers, and appealed to their public, was the unusual or impressive, scenes of foreign travel, monuments and wars. The common routine of everyday farming and rural life had few attractions for them except as an occasional source for a sentimental or glamorised subject.

After 1880, the adoption of the dry plate gave photographers the freedom to venture into the remote parts of the countryside without their darkroom tents. Public interest in rural subjects was now much greater for the rapid pace of change was making many sights, once commonplace, now bizarre. Thus to Sturt the flail appeared to be 'so obsolete and antiquated a thing as to be a novelty'. F. M. Sutcliffe was one of the earliest photographers of rural life to recognise the historical value of photography, for he realised that 'there are many things to be seen today which are not likely to be visible in ten years time, except in museums; some will not even get into the museums'. The technical limitations of the available equipment still tended to produce a predominance of static scenes and posed group photographs. These difficulties could often be overcome by techniques such as those employed by Sutcliffe, who requested his subjects to 'freeze' in the middle of their particular activity. Sutcliffe's use of arrested motion in his views of rural life on the North Yorkshire Moors and P. H. Emerson's use of actual motion in his famous picture of a Norfolk plough ('A stiff pull', published in 1888), pointed the way to the successful recording of working scenes in the countryside. Indeed by 1885 George Clausen was already using the 'snapshot' method to capture the labourer at work in the field.

The idea that photographs could be of value to document the social environment was shown by the appearance in 1877 of John Thomson's *Street Life in London* and by the work sponsored by the Society for Photographing the Relics of Old London, from 1874 to 1886. It was Sir Benjamin Stone who extended the concept of photographs as historical records to cover first individual countries and subsequently the whole country. His intention was 'to show those who will follow us, not only our buildings, but our everyday life, our manner and customs. Briefly, I have aimed at recording history with the camera, which, I think, is

5   Sheep washing at Ford End Farm, Ivinghoe, Buckinghamshire. c. 1900

the best way of recording it'. The Warwickshire Photographic Survey, inspired by Stone and established in 1890, together with subsequent surveys of other counties and the National Photographic Record Association (1897–1910), have left thousands of documented prints which include numerous illustrations of rural subjects. Stone's own personal interest was not confined to the photography of traditional customs and ceremonies, for which he is well known, but extended to a wide variety of other aspects of country life.

The requirements of commerce also led to the formation of documented series of record photographs. The agricultural engineering industry was quick to see the advantages that photographs offered in enabling them to publicise their products. A new design of implement or machine could be photographed outside the works, or more rarely at work in the field, and the image transferred directly to the wood block on which was engraved the illustration required for publicity purposes. The large firms who employed this technique soon began to assemble their photographs in bound volumes to form a continuous record of products.

The successful development of photographic printing at the end of the century enabled such firms to use photographs directly in their publicity catalogues. The trade journals of the agricultural engineering industry similarly made the change from line engravings so that photographs of the trials of the first successful British tractor, the Ivel, appeared in the pages of the *Implement and Machinery Review* in 1902 (see plate 42). Photographic printing also made possible the introduction of magazines illustrated by half-tone blocks. One of the outstanding examples was *Country Life* which first appeared in 1897 depicting farming, rural industries and the social and sporting life of the countryside in its pages.

The popularity of the picture postcard reached its zenith in the 20 years before 1914. It was common for private individuals to have their favourite pictures printed as postcards and many rural photographs have survived only in this form. The products of commercial firms, however, notably those of the company founded by Francis Frith, dominated the market. The increasing nostalgia felt by the urban population for a lost rural past led to the appearance of many favourite themes; the quiet village street, the cottage idyll, the old couple at the peaceful end of their days, the golden time of harvest, dinner break

for man and beast; all these subjects became the best-selling postcard clichés of the turn of the century.

The popular photograph is interesting for what it can tell us about the urban view of rural England, but is less valuable as an accurate image of the reality of country life as we know it from other sources. But every photograph contained in this selection reflects the photographer's ideas about the countryside and represents what he considered to be interesting, unusual or simply a confirmation of what he expected to find. One problem in interpreting these early photographs is to decide how representative they are of life in Victorian and Edwardian England. As the photographer usually speaks only through his camera we have to guess whether he thought he was taking something he regarded as rare or merely commonplace. This might, perhaps, be less of a problem if more photographs had been taken and more had survived. It is because they are so scarce compared to written sources that some care has to be attached to the reading of individual prints and when photographs lack adequate documentation, leaving persons, dates and often places unknown, that process is made more difficult. When the subject of the photograph can be correlated with known historical facts then it is often possible to decide whether it depicts a typical scene of life and work or has been taken because the subject was considered unusual.

Certainly, the pictorial interest and sentimental value attached to some subjects has led to their over-representation in material that survives. The picture of Thomas Butler (see plate 111) was probably added to the churches and cottages of the Warwickshire Photographic Survey because he made such a good subject and also closely conformed to the popular image of the agricultural worker (or 'peasant' as he was sometimes called). His image is, of course, a valuable record of the actual appearance of an old country dweller in 1891 from the top of his bowler to the irons of his clogs. There are many surviving pictures of Thomas Butler types, although very few as good. For every Thomas Butler, however, there were scores of younger labourers (looking less picturesque in clothes which were generally indistinguishable from those of the urban workmen of the day) who were virtually ignored by the photographers of this period. Contemporary observers had noted the passing of the distinctively rural dress. Thomas Hardy in his article *The Dorsetshire Labourer* which appeared in 1883 wrote of 'the rage for cloth clothes which possesses the labourers of today' and mentioned 'groups, who might be tailors or undertakers' men, for what they exhibit externally'. He found that 'out of a group of eight . . . only one wears corduroy trousers . . . the mechanic's "slop" has also been adopted; but a mangy old cloth coat is preferred'. We could therefore, assume that Thomas Butler was typical of only the older generation, who, wearing distinctive and old-fashioned clothes, tended to be photographed more often. Such pictures also helped to mould the popular image of agricultural workers so that here we might say reality recorded became myth confirmed.

Similar comments could be made about certain country characters. So many different pictures exist of the New Forest snake catcher 'Brusher' Mills that we might be misled into thinking that his profession had some real significance. He was probably its only practitioner and entirely untypical. Aged craftsmen in solitary woodland and village workshops and elderly lacemakers at their cottage doors were favourite subjects chiefly because they were thought to be the last survivors of a dying way of life. As such they excited the curiosity of the photographer and tempted him into a romantic rather than an analytical interpretation of rural change.

Likewise there was a bias towards the portrayal of certain agricultural operations. Every variety of harvest activity from haymaking to hop picking was exploited; a fact which may owe something to the kindness of summer weather but much more to the sense of nostalgia evoked by the sight of harvest gangs working together for a common purpose. Indeed, there was a preoccupation with the employ-ment of people in agriculture rather than with machinery. Thus, to my knowledge, there are far more photographs of scythesmen than there are of their machine competitors. Contemporary illus-trations of grass mowers and sail reapers are a rarity and yet those were a familiar sight after about 1870. It seems as if there was as much or even more of a fascination with the old and out-moded as with the new in farming so that the significance of mechanisa-tion can only be fully appreciated by reference to printed sources. The exception to this is perhaps provided by the many photographs showing the employment of steam on the farm and particularly the dramatic spectacle of the threshing set which appealed forcefully to the imagination of the nine-teenth-century photographer.

In contrast some important areas of rural life are thinly depicted by photographs. The impact of rail-ways on the countryside is poorly covered and scenes of domestic and social life are comparatively rare except for special occasions and ceremonies. It was obviously an art to photograph dark interiors so that poverty often went unnoticed. (Besides, few people wanted to see that image, preferring to think of the countryside as populated by sturdy and contented peasants.) All this would seem to suggest that photo-graphs cannot provide a complete picture of rural economy and society. Their usefulness as historical sources lies in an impression of the quality of life, and in the quantity of casual information that the photog-rapher, often in spite of himself, gives us; an immediate visual image that would take hundreds of words to describe, and then perhaps inadequately. Thus by means of a sequence of photographs it is possible to illustrate with precise detail the processes involved in the manufacturer of a gate hurdle; all the operations of the hay and corn harvest, of hop picking and drying and of the treatment of sheep in the summer from washing to dipping and marking. Photographs used in this book inform us that steam cultivation was undertaken at Acle, Norfolk with machinery manufactured in the early 1860s, that threshing with the flail was still practised on a Surrey farm at the turn of the century, that draught oxen were worked in modified horse harness in the northern Cotswolds before the First World War. Sometimes these facts are known from other sources, but occasionally a photograph may be the unique source for an activity, implement or costume in a particular place or at a certain date. And, even if this is not the case their appearance is exactly shown. The written evidence of the past will be amplified and modified, and our under-standing deepened. The photographer was the person on the spot at just the right time to record these moments of reality which assist us to set down the history of Victorian and Edwardian England with a confidence we dare not employ for any previous age.

6 Plank-sided Yorkshire wagon with a single draught pole at White House Farm, North Ferriby, in the East Riding of Yorkshire. Mr Arthur Baron, son of the tenant, is riding the horse; the labourer is 'Butt' Janson. *c.* 1895

Notes on photographers represented in this book

These local photographers, both amateur and professional never achieved the national prominence of Sutcliffe or Stone or shook the photographic establishment like Emerson. Their work may frequently be lacking in artistic quality but is most likely, together with the mass of material from unknown photographers, to represent the reality of rural life in Victorian and Edwardian England.

BASTIN, Alfred Harold (1875–1962). Lived in Reading for the greater part of his life. Nature writer and photographer, specialising in entomology. His rural photographs include a group showing woodland industries. The collection is held by the John Topham Picture Library. (Examples, plates 83–86, 121)

BOYER, William Henry (1827–1897). Professional photographer of Sandwich, Kent. His working career in this town from 1868–1896 has left a collection of about 3,000 glass negatives which form a valuable record of the output of an ordinary working photographer. This collection which is privately owned has only recently come to light, and a selection was shown at the Science Museum exhibition of 1975: *William Boyer—Photographer at The Chain*. (Examples, plates 2, 66, 81, 109)

CLAUSEN, Sir George (1852–1944). Painter of agricultural life and the labourer. His photographs of field workers taken near his home at Childwick Green, Hertfordshire between 1882 and 1885 were intended as studies for his paintings. The negatives are held by the Royal Photographic Society. (Examples, plates 12, 14, 112)

KNIGHT, John Henry (1847–1917). Lived at Weybourne House and subsequently Barfield near Farnham, Surrey. Inventor, farmer and motoring pioneer and writer on the motor car and electricity. His inventions included a hop ground digger, bricklaying machine, paraffin oil engine, and the two-seater car of 1895 (see plate 73). Knight's photographs were of his house and family, his inventions and scenes in Surrey and Hampshire. Collection at Farnham Museum. (Examples, plates 27, 29, 47, 73, 90)

PARKINSON, Frank (1873–1956). Son of a Spalding builder, who set up as a bulb grower at the nearby village of Pinchbeck. Amateur photographer of Lincolnshire. Collection at the Museum of Lincolnshire Life. (Example, plate 115)

PATTISON, J. W. *Rev.* (1853–1936). Held three County Durham livings in the Church of England from 1885 until his death. Some of his most interesting rural photographs were taken during his residence at St John's Chapel, Weardale. Collection at the North of England Open-Air Museum at Beamish Hall. (Examples, plates 17, 139)

POOL, Alfred (1864–1956). Inventor and engineer of Chipstable, Somerset, who also described himself as a photographic artist. His subjects were principally local people and buildings. Collection at the Museum of English Rural Life, University of Reading. (Example, plate 134)

READ, John (1884–1963). Professor of Chemistry at the Universities of Sydney and St Andrews successively and writer on chemistry, the history of chemistry and explosives. Founded the Camel Play Actors in 1910 to perform his own plays written in the dialect of his native Somerset. He hoped to inspire a revival of dialect in England, similar to that initiated by Cecil Sharp in folk song and dancing. Photographer of local people and farming scenes. Collection at the Museum of English Rural Life. (Examples, plates 31, 51, 63)

SIMS, Percy. Professional photographer of the early twentieth century. Produced his 'Country Life' series taken in the northern Cotswolds, as a postcard range. Part of collection still held at his original premises, now Packer's Studio, Chipping Norton. (Examples, plates 37, 52, 150)

TAUNT, Henry (1842–1922). Author, professional photographer and publisher of Oxford. Many of his photographs were sold as postcard series. Collections in several Thames Valley county libraries, the largest group being held by Oxfordshire. Taunt's work has become widely known since the publication of two books on him in 1973. (Example, plate 149)

For examples of work by F. M. Sutcliffe (1853–1941) see plate 7 and for Sir Benjamin Stone (1838–1914) see plate 65. They have both been the subject of recent books, as have P. H. Emerson (1856–1936) and Francis Frith (1822–1898).

The following photograph collections are held as part of the archives of agricultural engineering firms by the Museum of English Rural Life, University of Reading:

RANSOMES, SIMS & JEFFERIES LTD. OF IPSWICH. Manufacturers of ploughs, steam engines, threshing machines and lawn mowers. Started to compile a photographic record of their new products about 1856. The main sequence of the collection is contained in 27 bound volumes up to 1947. (Example, plate 41)

JOHN FOWLER & CO. (LEEDS) LTD. Manufacturers of steam cultivating equipment. The earliest photographs were taken by E. Wormald, a Leeds photographer, from about 1862 to 1886. The bound albums continued in various series until 1948. (Example, plate 28)

SUTTON & SONS LTD. Formerly of Reading. The firm took an interesting group of publicity photographs shortly after 1900. They illustrated luxuriant grass, wheat and mangold crops grown on local farms and were made into postcards used to acknowledge the receipt of orders at the Royal Seed Establishment, Reading. (Examples, plates 16, 20, 50)

Note on the commentaries

Places are located within the county boundaries which existed at the time of photography, and no account has been taken in the text of the local government reorganisation of 1974. For a few photographs the place is unknown but all are believed to have been taken in England (the book does not attempt to cover Scotland and Wales). Only a minority of photographs are precisely dated; otherwise an approximate estimate of the date has been established from internal evidence.

Traditional Farming

7   Raking out farmyard manure prior to spreading it over the field. The two-wheeled tip cart drawn by one or two horses was one of the most ubiquitous of all farm vehicles. Photographed by F. M. Sutcliffe on the North Yorkshire Moors, *c.* 1885

8   *Right* A corner of the farmyard at Will Hall near Alton, Hampshire. The cartshed houses three wagons of the Surrey type used in east Hampshire and on the right of the picture is a factory-built 'boat' wagon. In the shed behind the geese and hens is a stack of sheep cribs used for winter feeding of hay. *c.* 1900

9   *Right, below* Sheep feeding in the lambing yard attached to a farm. Note both the wattle hurdles for shelter and the stack of gate hurdles at the far end of the yard. On the left is a partially opened rick where the hay has been cut out with the hay knife. From a postcard, *c.* 1905

10 *Left* Team of six oxen hauling a turnwrest plough at Housedean Rise near Lewes, Sussex towards 1890. The ox boy is using a long wooden goad with a metal tip. By this date the employment of draught oxen in England was principally confined to a few localities in the southern downlands and the Cotswolds

11 *Below, left* The Kent turnwrest plough at Housedean Farm in April, 1888. This wooden plough was designed so that the wrest or mould-board and the coulter could be altered at the end of every furrow. Hence the furrow slice fell alternately to the left and right of the plough

12 *Right* A close study of hoeing. This and picture No. 14 were taken by George Clausen near his home at Childwick Green, St Albans between 1882 and 1885. They are probably the earliest unposed photographs of labourers at work in the field.

13 *Below* Hoeing between cabbages at Cippenham Court Farm, near Slough, Buckinghamshire about 1910

14 A mower photographed by George Clausen

15 Haymakers turning windrows of hay. From a postcard of 1906

Haymaking

16 When completely dry the hay is raked into cocks which are amalgamated to form windrows for loading on to cart or wagon. This large group of field workers is taking in the harvest on the Lockinge Estate on the Berkshire Downs about 1905. A horse rake is also in use to supplement the work of the hand rakers. Photograph taken by Sutton & Sons, the seedsmen of Reading

17 *Top* Gathering the hay into pikes (or large cocks as in the field beyond) with a gate sweep at Riggside, St John's Chapel, Weardale, Co. Durham. The hay harvest, to provide the winter's livestock fodder, was often the most important of the year on northern hill farms. Photograph by Rev. J. W. Pattison of St John's Chapel about 1910

18 *Above* Henry Reynolds' labourers at Burgh, Suffolk about 1890. These scythes, used in the wheat harvest, have wooden cradles attached to help lay the crop for ease of gathering

19 Sharpening the bagging hook during wheat harvesting in Herefordshire. The corn was held by a crooked stick and the stalks severed by means of a slashing action of this large, heavy hook. The tool which had partly replaced the reap hook and serrated sickle had itself been largely superseded by the scythe. *c.* 1900

20 A harvest company cutting wheat with the scythe and gathering the crop, about 1905. At this date the scythe would normally be employed only to open a field for the reaper or binder, or to cut a badly laid crop. Photograph by Sutton and Sons of Reading

21 Wagon in the harvest field at Berwick, Sussex. Both these horses are wearing leather housen dropped flat, the normal practice in wet weather to protect the area between the collar and the cart saddle or back band. *c.* 1890

22 A similar wagon near Plumpton, Sussex. It will be seen how the use of these crudely made poles (in place of the more usual 'ladders') greatly increased its carrying capacity at hay and corn harvest. *c.* 1890

23 Stacking from a 'boat' wagon at Waddon, now part of Croydon, during the 1907 harvest. The picture clearly illustrates the difference between the trace harness of the lead horse and the shaft harness of the shaft horse. From a postcard

24 *Below, left* Threshing in the open air at Brook, Albury, Surrey. The larger chaff is removed from the threshed grain with the riddle or sieve, seen in the background, prior to machine winnowing. The straw is being twisted into a rope used for many farm purposes; Mr Holt the farmer is the band feeder on the right-hand side. Hand threshing was becoming an unusual sight by the time this picture was taken about 1900

25 *Below* Threshing with the flail about 1885. In the background is a hand-operated winnowing machine

Mechanised Farming

26 A Kitson & Hewitson engine at Acle, Norfolk. The cultivator has reached the end of its run before it is turned and the engine and anchor moved along the headland for the next run. The cultivator, employed to stir the soil rather than completely invert it, and to cut the weed roots, was the most popular implement used in steam cultivation. Owing to the expense of purchasing the equipment it was normally operated for hire by specialist contractors, in this case Alfred Watson of Thorpe, Norwich. *c.* 1870

27 *Right* The factory-made iron plough was replacing the locally constructed wooden beam plough throughout the country. This example was manufactured by Ransomes, Sims & Jefferies of Ipswich. The hops in the background are pole trained. Taken near Farnham, Surrey by J. H. Knight, *c.* 1890

28 One of the earliest photographs of steam cultivation, taken by E. Wormald of Leeds. The engine was built for John Fowler & Co., by Kitson & Hewitson about 1862, shortly before the company's own Steam Plough Works were established. This was the single engine system in which a balance plough was hauled backwards and forwards between the winding drum, under the engine's boiler, and a movable anchor located on the headland of the field. The distance between engine and anchor was shortened for the purposes of the photograph. From the archives of John Fowler & Co., (Leeds) Ltd

29 The Suffolk type of steerage drill, near Farnham. This implement was expensive in use of labour, here employing four horses, two men and a boy. The man at the front of the drill held the steerage handle and kept the small fore wheels in the track of the large wheels so that the rows of corn were drilled perfectly straight, aiding use of the horse hoe. The man behind ensured that the chutes did not become blocked. This particular drill was manufactured by Richard Garrett & Sons of Leiston, Suffolk. *c.* 1890

30 *Right* Horse-drawn crop sprayer at Cippenham Court Farm, near Slough about 1910. The chemical was probably Bordeaux mixture of copper sulphate and lime, commonly used against potato fungus

31 *Right, below* Passing cider to the driver of the mowing machine, which superseded the scythe for cutting hay. Photograph by John Read, near Wincanton, Somerset, *c.* 1900

32 *Left* Stacking hay, using the horse-operated crane, in the north of England. The apparatus consisted of the single braced wooden pole, the jib and grab fork. As the horse walked forward he pulled up the truss of hay by means of a line running through a pulley block. *c.* 1900

33 *Left, below* Harvesting oats in Cumberland. This is a manual delivery reaping machine, very similar in principle to some of the earliest effective reapers of the mid-nineteenth century. The corn to be cut was collected on to the knife blades by the hand-held rake and tipped off the platform by a lever as the cut sheaf accumulated. The women in the foreground are binding the sheaves with straw for stooking. *c.* 1900

34 Self-raking or sail reaper, the typical reaping machine of the late nineteenth century before the introduction of the self-binder. A large labour force was still required to bind and stook the sheaves. From a postcard, *c.* 1905

35 *Left* Harvesting oats at Slinfold, Sussex, with a self-binding reaper. A far more expensive and complicated piece of machinery than the sail reaper, the self-binder offered considerable economies in labour and remained in use until superseded by the combine harvester. From a post-card, *c.* 1910

36 *Left, below* Stacking with the straw elevator, driven by portable horse gear, at Yarnton, Oxfordshire, 1909. The wagon is of the south midland type

37 A portable steam engine made by Brown & May of Devizes driving a Gibbons & Robinson threshing machine from the Vale of the White Horse Ironworks, Wantage, Berkshire. Note the shafts by means of which the engine was hauled by horse from farm to farm. Photograph by Percy Sims of Chipping Norton, Oxfordshire, *c.* 1910

38 *Overleaf* A larger and more advanced type of portable engine manufactured by Davey Paxman of Colchester, driving a Nalder & Nalder threshing machine from Challow, Wantage, Berkshire. Photograph from the archives of Nalder & Nalder Ltd, *c.* 1900

39 The self-moving traction engine
was the successor of the portable
as the power source to drive the
threshing machine. On the right of
this picture taken at Gipps Farm,
Newick, Sussex, are the water and
coal carts which attended on the
engine. *c.* 1900

40 A set of threshing tackle, towed by a Clayton & Shuttleworth agricultural traction engine, entering Semer Lodge, Semer, Suffolk. The equipment was owned by Philip Gage, a farmer of Chelsworth. *c.* 1910

42   The Ivel tractor drawing an adapted Samuelson mower near Biggleswade, Bedfordshire in 1902. The inventor, Dan Albone of Biggleswade is walking behind the tractor on the left. The tractor received high praise in all practical trials but its development was curtailed by Albone's sudden death in 1906. Photograph from the *Implement and Machinery Review*

41 *Left* Ransomes & Sims' works team of Suffolk Punches and their plough that won four out of six competitions at the Newcastle Royal Show of 1884. The Newcastle prize plough was perhaps the peak of development reached by the iron single-furrow horse plough, an implement widely used in ploughing matches ever since. Much of the success at the show was no doubt due to the skill of James Barker, the company's champion ploughman, seen at the handles. Mr. J. E. Ransome stands on the right of the group of four. From the archives of Ransomes, Sims & Jefferies Ltd, of Ipswich

43 A patent digging machine, designed for use in hop grounds, developed by J. H. Knight from 1875 to 1878. It was demonstrated on Knight's farm at Badshot, near Farnham, the version shown here being built by J. & F. Howard of Bedford. As the machine was drawn across the field, by means of a cable and a portable steam engine, the forks went in and out of the ground at high speed. It was invented because Knight was unable to obtain enough men to dig his hop grounds, but he discontinued its use after a few years. The photograph was used to engrave the publicity leaflet for the digger

Hops and Fruit

44   Stacks of hop poles before the
growing season at Will Hall Farm, near
Alton, Hampshire. c. 1900

45 Mr & Mrs Knight stringing the hop poles at Henry Chalcraft's Amery Farm, near Alton in 1902. This was the Butcher system of wirework in which the overhead system of wires supported by poles carried the strings along which the hop bines were trained

46 The same hop ground ready for picking. The baskets (graduated inside by lines marking each bushel) are laid out for the pickers to begin. On this farm they took about two hours to fill a seven-bushel basket, earning $1\frac{1}{2}$d–$2\frac{1}{2}$d per bushel

47 Interior of a hop kiln near Farnham, showing the operation of the hop press. The dried hops were rammed very tightly into the large pockets in which they were transported and which weighted 1½ cwt when full. The pocket was suspended from a metal framework and hung down to the floor below. Photograph by J. H. Knight, *c.* 1890

48 *Right* These hops at Mordants Farm, Crowle, Worcestershire have been picked into bins, consisting of a wooden framework covered by sacking. The measurer scoops them into the bushel basket, and after each bushel has been entered by the 'booker' it is emptied into the loosely packed poke or green bag (containing ten or twelve bushels) for transport to the kiln. *c.* 1905.

49 *Right, below* A cherry picking gang in the west Hertfordshire cherry growing district at Red Heath Farm, Croxley Green. The men were employed by Harry Aldridge, a fruiterer of High Wycombe, Buckinghamshire, who annually purchased the crop from these large and well-established trees. The 80-feet-high fruit-picking ladders were designed for stability and ease of movement from tree to tree. Note the two different sorts of basket in use, the one for picking into, attached to the ladder by a hook, and the other, the half bushel, for the transport of the crop. *c.* 1895

Livestock

50 Shredding mangolds for cattle in a root pulper. The crop was grown by J. Thorp of Binfield, Berkshire and the photograph taken to advertise their Golden Tankard mangolds by Sutton & Sons of Reading, *c.* 1905

51 *Right* Carter and his horses near Wincanton, Somerset. Photograph by John Read, *c.* 1900

52 *Right, below* Homecoming plough team in the northern Cotswolds. These shorthorns were worked in the modified horse harness which here replaced the traditional wooden yoke (see plate 10). Photograph by Percy Sims, *c.* 1910

53 *Left* Milking in Cornwall about 1875

54 The milker is now wearing a white coat but conditions in the farmyard are still unhygienic. Taken at Lower East Farm, East Meon, Hampshire, *c*. 1900

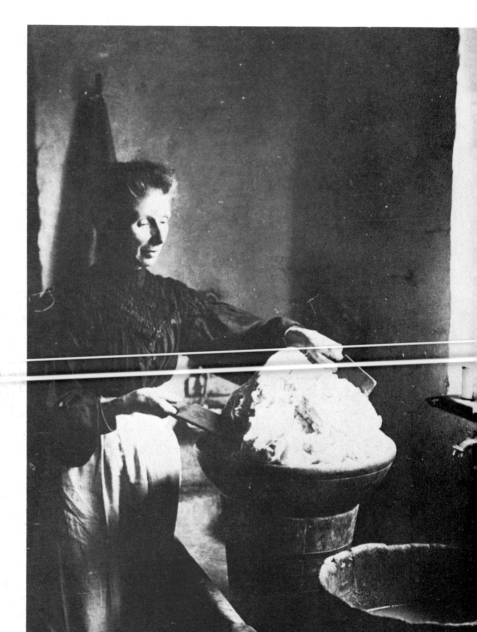

55 Buttermaking inside the farm dairy at Riplington Farm, East Meon, about 1910. This shows the butter at the stage when it was washed under water with the aid of wooden pats to remove the buttermilk. The wooden dairying vessels of both turned and coopered construction have not yet been replaced by those of earthenware or tin and the stone sink is still in use. But for the piped water supply the methods could be those of a century before

56 Loading a sledge with bracken in the Lake District fells to use as winter bedding for livestock. *c.* 1890

57 *Right* Penning sheep at Acland Barton, near Landkey, Devon. *c.* 1895

58 Sheep washing at Rydal, Westmorland. The Herdwick sheep are thrown into the water and guided by a pole to the head of the pool, created by damming up a stream. A higher market price could be obtained for clean wool. *c.* 1900

59 Sheep were sheared about two weeks after washing when the new wool had had time to raise the fleece from the skin. This gang was employed at Hackwood Farm, Winslade, Hampshire. *c.* 1900

60 Dipping sheep after shearing at Cippenham Court Farm, near Slough about 1910. The dip gave protection against scab, parasites and attacks from flies. The wooden dipping tub shown here was manufactured by Fletcher Bros. of Grimsby, whose dipping apparatus won first prize in the competitive trials at the Royal Show of 1894

61 Marking the clipped sheep with an iron dipped in hot pitch at Redmire, Mungrisedale, Cumberland. It was particularly important to establish ownership in hill areas where flocks ranged over a wide area of countryside. *c.* 1900

62 Feeding the fowls at Riplington Farm, East Meon, Hampshire about 1910. The poultry house is on staddle stones to prevent access by vermin

63 Berkshire pigs at Motcombe, Dorset about 1895. The breed, then widespread, is now rare. A John Read photograph

Transport

64 An elegant wagonette outside Leeds Castle, Kent. The vehicle was perhaps used here to take guests to and from the station, Leeds being five miles from Maidstone and seven miles from Headcorn stations. *c.* 1900

65 *Right* Farm wagons carrying hop pickers from the Black Country to the Worcestershire hop gardens. The photograph was taken at Witley, Worcestershire by Sir Benjamin Stone in 1896

66 *Right, below* In addition to its harvest function the farm wagon was employed for road transport, including the carriage of grain. This wagon is of the Kent type and the horses are wearing fly netting. Photograph by William Boyer of Sandwich, about 1885.

67 Wheeled traffic outside the Red Lion Inn at Thursley, Surrey about 1900. Among the vehicles may be seen an Ind Coope covered brewer's dray, a light wagonette, and a small livestock cart fitted with a crank axle to bring its body closer to the ground. Note also the pre-tarmacadam road surface and the galvanised iron 'Jubilee Room' on the right

68 Small carrier's cart at Porthcurnow, St Levan parish, Cornwall. A network of short-distance carriers covered the country, filling in the gaps in the railway network and providing a means of public communication between villages and their neighbouring market towns. A small cart such as this would carry only unaccompanied goods. *c.* 1900

69 Delivery cart, owned by Savage
& Parsons, grocers and bakers of East
Meon, Hampshire. The deliveryman
is Charlie Merritt. Local bakers had
extended their delivery areas at the
end of the nineteenth century as the
practice of home baking declined.
c. 1900

70 *Left* One of the ploughing engines owned by the Oxfordshire Steam Ploughing Company of Cowley, Oxford after an accident in 1911. Accidents to steam road vehicles were usually spectacular, drawing the inevitable idle crowd and the prompt arrival of the local photographer to record the event

71 *Left, below* Fast passenger transport between town and country, for those who could afford the fares

72 Goods traffic at Stoke by Clare station, Suffolk on the Great Eastern Railway towards the end of the nineteenth century. Railways gave hitherto remote areas the opportunity to send bulk quantities of agricultural produce to distant markets and receive supplies of commodities like coal at far higher speeds and a relatively cheaper rate than had been possible by road or water transport

73 At the photographer's request everyone will maintain their motor vehicles. J. H. Knight is standing to the left of the car that he built in 1895, claimed to be the first petrol-driven two-seater car in England. It was the only British vehicle to be demonstrated at the Crystal Palace motor show of 1896. In 1902 Knight wrote how 'after a few months the owner gets a sort of affection for the car, almost as if it were a living being. When running at speed the driver sees very little of the scenery on the road, except for straight ahead, for a couple of seconds' inattention to steering might cause a serious accident'. Probably taken at Knight's home, Barfield, near Farnham shortly before 1910.

74 A motor and cycle dealer's premises at Overton, Hampshire before the First World War. The motor vehicles brought with them a requirement for a new kind of engineering skill in villages and market towns. It will be seen how early the sale, repair and maintenance of such vehicles, including the retailing of petrol, had begun to alter the appearance of small country towns.

Markets and Shops

75 Farmers' wagons and carriers' vans outside the White Hart Inn, High East Street, Dorchester. The photograph must have been taken after the turn of the century because of the sign advertising carriage and motor works and a garage. It was from this inn that the 'Longpuddle' carrier's van set out in Thomas Hardy's short story, *A Few Crusted Characters*

76 *Right* A Lake District farmer on his way to market with a consignment of geese. *c*. 1890.

77 Mr T. T. Iveson, auctioneer, at a farm sale at Whittonstall, Northumberland in 1892

78 Mr William Staley of Underhurth Farm, Forest in Teesdale, Co. Durham, taken at Middleton in Teesdale in 1905 after he had walked seven miles with his Shorthorn cow to the railway station. She must have been regarded as a fine cow for she fetched £25, a high price for the time

79 Cabbages loaded on to the market wagon for London at William Bond's farm, Ilford, Essex. *c.* 1895

80 *Left* Inside the wholesale fruit and vegetable market at St Martin's Lane, Birmingham at 8.00 a.m. in June 1901. This produce would have arrived in such wagons from the market garden areas surrounding the Birmingham conurbation.

81 *Right* Shops owned by the Austin family with their staff and delivery cart, probably in the Kent village of Eastry. The influence of Huntley & Palmer's biscuits appears to be paramount in the window display; they were one of the first nationally known brand names in the grocery trade. Photograph by William Boyer of Sandwich about 1887

82 A display of wares outside J. Brownscombe's saddle, collar and harness maker's premises at High Bickington, Devon. This business was involved in all branches of the saddler's trade, producing cart and plough harness and collars, in addition to riding saddles. *c.* 1900

Rural Industries

83 Stripping bark from a felled oak in a Kentish coppice. The bark was removed to the height a man could reach before felling and the rest stipped off with the barking iron when the tree was on the ground. Photograph by Harold Bastin of Reading, *c* 1910

84 *Right* Loading dried bark for transport out of the woods on its way to the tanneries. The oak bark trade virtually died out after the First World War when new products were substituted for the tanning process.

The inscription on the side of this wagon tells us that it was owned by Archibald C. Norman, Oakley Farm, Bromley, Kent. Photograph by Harold Bastin, *c.* 1910

85 Winter work in a wood grown on the system of coppice with standards. The standards were mature trees grown for timber and coppice was the term given to planted woodland periodically harvested, every eight to twenty years, according to species. A use was found for every scrap of material down to the last twig. Here the different types of wood are placed into separate stacks, the bundles of bavins for firing ovens and kilns and the poles for supporting hops, beans and peas and as raw material for the manufacture of other woodland products. Photograph by Harold Bastin, c. 1910

86 Wastewood in woodland areas difficult of access might be burnt on the spot to produce charcoal. This is the encampment of a group of itinerant charcoal burners, probably i the New Forest. During the three to five days the clamp was burning it needed watching day and night, henc the construction of temporary shelters on the site. Charcoal was still used in the manufacture of gunpowder and for the smelting of some iron ores in the Furness district. Photograph by Harold Bastin, c. 1910

87 Stacks of turned legs drying outside the chair bodger's huts in Buckinghamshire, 1902. At this time 50,000 people were employed in the furniture industry in and around High Wycombe, the backs and seats of the Windsor chairs being generally manufactured in Wycombe itself. The output of a team of two bodgers per day might amount to two gross legs and stretchers, giving them eight shillings between them. Unlike coppice plantations this required the use of mature timber in naturally regenerated woodlands.

88 Using the pole lathe to turn the roughly shaped legs and stretcher pieces. The pole acted as a giant spring, being attached to a foot treadle by a cord which passed around the leg to be turned. Pressing the treadle caused the leg to revolve at great speed as the lathe tools were used on it. The huts were erected by the chair bodgers themselves and were constructed from beech saplings and canvas and thatched with straw

89 Gate hurdle making at the Home Farm on the Ashridge Estate at Little Gaddesden, Hertfordshire. The pole is being cleft with the froe (or cleaving axe) as it is held in the brake. The hurdle maker pushes the froe downwards and draws the pole towards him to lengthen the split. *c.* 1910

90 *Right* Gate hurdle maker and his temporary shelter in a coppice in west Surrey or Hampshire. The hut is of cleft wood, roofed with bark peelings. J. H. Knight photograph, *c.* 1900

91 *Right, below* Cuthbert Westbrook making wattle hurdles on the Herriard Estate in Hampshire about 1900. The uprights were set into slots in a wooden frame and the horizontal rods woven into them, both cleft and natural hazel being used in one hurdle. In the background may be seen a stack of cut hazel poles ready for use and a pile of finished hurdles which are being left to season for a few weeks. Gate and wattle hurdles were used in the south of England as portable enclosures to fold sheep on pastures and in the lambing yard, the wattle variety giving more protection from the weather (see plate 9)

92 *Left* Preparation of white willow for basket making. The woman and boy are stripping the bark from the rods by drawing them between steel blades set into the brakes. The man is stacking bundles of peeled rods ready for the despatch to the basket maker. *c.* 1890

93 *Left, below* Spale basket making in the north or west midlands. These baskets, woven from split oak, were used for domestic, agricultural and industrial purposes in the midlands and the north. On the right the oak 'spelks' are being trimmed on the shaving horse with a draw knife; on the left the thin pliable strips, having been immersed in water, are interwoven to form a basket. The basket making is here combined with the manufacture of besoms which are held in the foot-operated vice for tying. *c.* 1905

94 *Below* The timber carriage used to transport felled timber out of the woods is seen here crossing the Severn at Hampton Loade, Upper Arley, Worcestershire in 1892

95 Before the introduction of power machinery the pit saw was the normal method of cutting a tree into level lengths. The top sawyer directed the saw's action and had the hard task of pulling the saw up on every stroke, the bottom sawyer, or pit man, had less responsibility but the necessity of suffering a rain of sawdust on him. Photograph from the album of Alec Walter, a plough-wright from Shalbourne, Wiltshire

96 Brown's sawmill at Mitford, Northumberland, driven by a traction engine, with water cart in the background. Photograph from the Mitford Collection at Northumberland Record Office, *c.* 1910

97 The production of farm and commercial carts in the lower workshop of Humphries & Sons Wagon Works at Chippenham, Wiltshire about 1910. Among the craftsmen and employees are Mr Francis Humphries, son of the founder, who is holding a wheel to the left of his daughter, Phyllis, and the blacksmith with his apprentice standing in the left centre with their hammers over their shoulders

98 The finished product of a small wheelwright's business. A newly built cart for J. Rose of Sawtry, Huntingdonshire, built by W. Barfield of Sawtry in 1898. Decorative painting, including the spectacle design frequently found on the front boards of carts and wagons of eastern England, was clearly a speciality of this firm

100 *Right* Inside a blacksmith's forge in the Rothbury area of Northumberland. *c.* 1910

99 Binding a metal tyre on to a wheel at Clanfield, Hampshire. Most village blacksmiths, as well as specialist wheelwrights, had a tyring platform outside their forge, for this was a task which overlapped the skills of both occupations. The wheel was clamped on to the platform, the circular iron tyre heated until red hot and then placed over the wheel and rammed home, being immediately cooled with a large quantity of water so that it would contract fast against the wooden rim, binding the whole assembly together. Retyring was frequently required in summer when the wood shrank and the tyres worked loose. *c.* 1910

101 Thatching at Kenchester, Herefordshire about 1905. Long straw thatching, like straw plaiting, required the use of good undamaged straw, preferably reaped by hand and frequently obtained from the path cut round a field to open it up for the reaper of binder. The thatcher is combing the straw down with a side rake to give an even finish to the surface

102 Women plaiting straw at Tring, Hertfordshire on a market day towards the end of the nineteenth century. They are perhaps waiting to sell their finished work to dealers and buy fresh supplies of prepared straw from them. The bundles of straw were held under their left arms and as each straw was drawn out it was moistened with the lips and plaited with a number of other straws. This was a major cottage industry over a large area of Bedfordshire, Buckinghamshire, Hertfordshire and a part of Essex, its most important finished product being the straw hat

103 A Buckinghamshire lace maker in 1898. The pattern was marked out by pins stuck into the design traced on parchment, and the threads intertwined by means of bobbins made of wood or bone. The winder on the table behind the worker was used to wind skeins of thread on to the bobbin ready for use on the pillow. The Buckinghamshire Pillow Point Lace Industry, to whom the photograph belonged, was set up as part of an attempt to revive this cottage industry, by teaching the craft and marketing the finished lace

104 Robert John Snare (1835–98), flintmaster of Brandon, Suffolk in 1886. He is seen here quartering a large block of flint before breaking it into smaller pieces (flaking) for striking gun flints (knapping). The flint is rested on the leather knee pad and the iron hammer is allowed to fall on it so that it splits along its natural line of cleavage. A one-sided flint miner's pick has been placed in the photograph on the right. It was usual to work at the entrance of the hut in summer to get the benefit of the light. At this period about 80,000 flints a week were being produced by the industry for export to areas using flint-lock muskets and as strike-a-lights

105 Quarry workers using mallets and chisels to split stone into smaller sized blocks. Some weather protection is provided by the simple lean-to shelter. The exact location of this quarry, in or near Buckinghamshire, is not known but it seems likely that it was a temporary site established after a stratum of suitable limestone had been located under the surface. *c.* 1900

106 *Right* A country potter throwing plant pots at Wrockmore Hill pottery, Buckinghamshire in 1909. Small rural potteries, producing a limited range of products such as these coarse redware plant pots, were rapidly going out of business before the competition of factory-made products

Rural Workers

107 Sheep shearers at the farm of James Andrews, farmer and hop grower of West Court, Binsted, Hampshire, throwing up their hats at the end of shearing here. The work was frequently carried out by itinerant groups who would form up for the season and contract with the farmer to shear his flock on a piecework basis. The penny-farthing tricycle and the bicycle suggest the increased mobility becoming available to better paid workers at this time. *c.* 1890

108 *Right* Staff on Thomas Woodman's farm at Littlecote, a hamlet of Stewkley parish, Buckinghamshire. This photograph, taken about 1880, illustrates a period of transition in costume when the smock, although now going out of fashion, is still worn by half of the men present; the wide range of headgear is also noteworthy

109 Labourers with jugs of beer outside Caroline Gibbs' beerhouse at Elmstone, near Ash, Kent. Photograph by William Boyer of Sandwich about 1882

110 The farmer, his relations and servants at Northern Wood Farm, Blofield, Norfolk towards 1880. Mr Waters, who purchased the farm in 1832, is third from the right. His niece is standing next to him with her son holding a gun on the extreme right. On the left stand the dairymaid and the farm's two horsemen, in the jerseys sometimes worn by Norfolk labourers

111 Thomas Butler, labourer at Knowle, Warwickshire. The photograph was taken by James Simkins with a 15-second exposure as part of the Warwickshire Photographic Survey in December 1891 and was entitled 'Warwickshire peasant'. Thomas Butler seems well protected from cold and damp with his layers of clothing, leather gaiters and clogs, the latter a type of footwear rarely worn by agricultural labourers of this period

112 Field woman with shawl and sacking apron pausing in her task of trimming turnips. Taken by George Clausen, near St Albans, between 1882 and 1885

113 In the centre is Mr William Hall of Bradleyburn Farm, Wolsingham in Weardale, Co. Durham, *c.* 1900. The small upland farms of the northern hills were worked by both the men and women of the family; other farm servants, if they existed, would often live in

114 Harvesters taking 'beavers' in Suffolk. *c.* 1895

115 Child gleaners in Lincolnshire. The opportunity of gleaning the harvest provided an additional source of winter food for the family and their pig or poultry. The few sacks of corn gathered by women and children were won only at the expense of considerable toil. In the view of Richard Jefferies, 'Gleaning—poetical gleaning—is the most unpleasant and uncomfortable of labour, tedious, slow, back-aching work'. Frank Parkinson's photographs of gleaners won a prize at the Nottingham Photographic Society's Exhibition of 1902

116 Another view of harvesters at dinner, taken at Ashdown Farm, near Bradworthy, Devon. The man sporting the bow tie in the centre of the group appears to belong to a higher social class. *c.* 1900

117 Shepherd carrying wattle hurdles and part of his flock, near Alton, Hampshire. *c.* 1900

118 A tea party given for willow workers at Lower Knapp, North Curry, Somerset. Mr Dare the farmer and willow grower is standing in the centre of the picture. *c.* 1900

119 Theobold, a rabbit catcher who came from near Methwold, Norfolk to Mr Phillip Gardner's Conington Hall Estate in Cambridgeshire every year. He sent ferrets on a line down the burrows and if the rabbit did not bolt out of another hole he would dig down with the long-handled spade at spots where the ferret may have driven it. Bolting rabbits would be caught by nets placed over the burrows or by one of the dogs. These are Theobold's lurcher and fox terrier and a spaniel belonging to Mr Gardner. *c.* 1895

120 Woodman photographed by Frank Howard of the Amateur Photographic Field Club about 1900. The timber carriage in the background is adapted to take items like hop poles

122 Some farm labourers were victimised for their part in strikes or membership of their newly established unions after farmers had organised themselves to resist wage demands. This photograph shows villagers watching evictions at Milborne St Andrew, Dorset in April 1874. It is interesting to see a high proportion of the village's inhabitants assembled together. The presence of the musicians and the cheerful expressions on some of the participants give the occasion a slightly more festive appearance than might have been expected from the nature of the proceedings

123 *Right, above* Some members of the evicted families and their possessions at Milborne St Andrew. In spite of these setbacks, and the ultimate failure of the National Agricultural Labourers' Union, Thomas Hardy considered that an average rise of three shillings a week in wages (or between 30 and 40 per cent) had been gained in Dorset, one of the worst paid counties in England

124 *Right* The new agricultural unionism of the twentieth century. Some of the audience at Swanton Morley, Norfolk when George Edwards visited the village to re-form the union branch as part of the Eastern Counties Agricultural Labourers' Union

Domestic Life

125 Mother and child outside a cottage at Upton, Berkshire. The building may or may not have been clean and comfortable inside; that depended on the number, means and inclinations of the occupants. C. M. Chapman reporting for the 1893 *Royal Commission on Labour* found that 'There is cause for complaint also at . . . Upton . . . but more often from the natural decay of old cottages than from bad construction'. Cage birds were commonly seen hanging outside country cottages at this time. A photograph by Frank Howard of the Amateur Photographic Field Club, *c.* 1900

126 Washing outside cottages near Penzance, Cornwall. Although a posed photograph it does give some idea of the labour and equipment associated with the women's washing day. *c.* 1900

127 The two daughters of Mr Buggey, a worker at Earl Brownlow's Ashridge Estate on the Hertfordshire/ Buckinghamshire border. *c.* 1895

128 *Right* Edith Hawkins (born 1879) in the kitchen at Pitstone Green farmhouse, Buckinghamshire.

129 *Right, below* Mr and Mrs Hall at home in Gresham, Norfolk about 1880. The original wide fireplace has been partially filled in by a small cast-iron range with a baking oven. On the left is a revolving butter churn

130 Preparing to kill a pig (believed to be of the now extinct Cumberland breed) at Rookhope, Weardale, Co. Durham. Mr Thomas Oliver, the pig killer holding the rope, was also a lead smelter at Rookhope Smelt Mill. The pot into which the animal's blood was drained may be seen behind the axe. *c.* 1910

131 The local pig killer with his spring cart containing the pig form on which the carcase was laid. Taken outside the Raven public house at Great Gap, Ivinghoe parish, Buckinghamshire. *c.* 1900

132 A donkey wheel acting as the power source to raise water from a large and deep well. It remained in use in large houses, farms and inns for it was uneconomic to install a steam engine where a continuous supply of water was not required. This wheel was located at Dummer, Hampshire. *c.* 1900

133 Gipsy King Hedges and his family at Teston Green, Kent. The van is of the Reading type and is very much more ornate than the partly covered vehicle standing next to it. *c.* 1900

Community Services

134 Interior of a Somersetshire chapel with harvest festival offerings. The harvest festival service was a creation of the last half of the nineteenth century. Its introduction coincided with the spread of mechanisation and was ironically followed by the onset of the depression in arable farming. Harvest celebrations had previously been entirely secular and often rowdy occasions. *c.* 1890

135 Inside a Quaker meeting house in Hampshire. Note the two rushlight holders standing on the table. *c.* 1900

136 Officially directed games at Long Marston school, Hertfordshire during May Day celebrations which also included dancing around a maypole. This was a revival of a custom whose only genuine survival was the children's May garland procession still held in some parishes. *c.* 1910

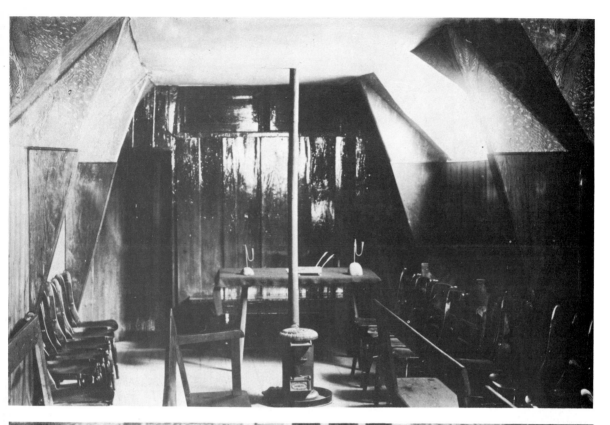

137 Helpers and patients at the Christmas tea in the Workhouse Infirmary at Wimborne Minster, Dorset, 1910. The chaplain in the background is probably the Rev. George Henry Billington. Conditions in many infirmaries were now improved and the introduction of old age pension had provided an alternative prospect to indoor relief in the workhouses (soon to be renamed Poor Law Institutions) for the aged poor

138 A posed photograph to celebrate Pension Day, 6 January 1909, outside Wickhambrook Post Office, Suffolk. Those aged over 70 received five shillings a week provided their means did not exceed £21 a year (or rather more than eight shillings a week). There was grumbling in the contemporary press about the acceptance of pensions by old people who had large sums in the Post Office Savings Bank and some rather querulous surprise at the numbers who applied for them. It was feared that the receipt of state aid would undermine the desire of these septugenarians to perform their 'honest toil'

139 Leaving school in Co. Durham. Photograph by Rev. J. W. Pattison, *c.* 1900

140 Staff outside the post office at Hartest, Suffolk. The district was served by a postmistress, a parcel delivery cart and driver, two other regular postmen and five auxiliary letter carriers. *c.* 1910

141 Electioneering at East Tisted, Hampshire. William Wickham, the candidate supported, was returned as Conservative member for the East Hampshire (Petersfield) division in the general election of 1892, beating the Gladstonian Liberal, J. Bonham Carter, by 3,912 to 3,008 votes. In the 1895 election he was returned unopposed but died two years later. The 1884 Reform Act effectively extended the franchise to all male householders in the countryside so that county members now had occasion to solicit the vote of the rural labourer

Relaxation

142 The countryside as a place for open-air relaxation. A picnic party, probably in Herefordshire, about 1902

143 A meet of the North Warwickshire fox hounds at Claverton, 18 November 1904. Photograph taken as part of the Warwickshire Photographic Survey

144 Loading the game wagon with the results of a morning's pheasant shoot at Studley Royal, in the West Riding of Yorkshire. It was organised as a two-day shoot for six guns by the Marquis of Ripon in 1901

145 The village cricket team of Garsington, Oxfordshire in 1898

146 *Right, above* The village band at Standlake, Oxfordshire outside Florey's farm at Brighthampton, Oxfordshire. Strings were the backbone of this band, the two brass players in uniform may have also belonged to other local brass bands. *c.* 1900

147 *Right* Club day at Sibford, Oxfordshire. This view shows the procession of the Sibford Friendly Society, formed up to march to the church with the choir, vicar and local M.P., the brass band and the members with their staffs. *c.* 1910

48 *Left* The Ilmington Morris dancers, Warwickshire, performing the shepherd's hey dance. The 'horse' stands upright and has the circular image of the animal attached to him. The Ilmington team was disbanded in 1867 but reconstituted about twenty years later and it was this group, which included four members of the original team, that survived long enough for their dances to be recorded by Cecil Sharp. *c.* 1895

149 *Left, below* Outside the George Inn at Radley, Berkshire during the beating of the bounds. The original purpose of this ceremony was to perambulate a legal boundary in a way guaranteed to impress its location on the inhabitants of a parish. It was continued in some places as a traditional observance. A Henry Taunt photograph, *c.* 1895

150 An ox team from the Springhill Estate, Broadway, Worcestershire carrying the May Queen and her attendants at Stratford-upon-Avon fair. Photograph by Percy Sims, *c.* 1910

151 Another leisure use for working farm teams was supplying transport for Sunday School outings. This wagon headed a convoy from Kirby Moorside in the North Riding of Yorkshire in 1903 and was lent by John Cussons of Edston. It is of the small type used in North Yorkshire and is fitted with shafts instead of the central draught pole more usual in this area. Full harness decorations are worn for the occasion, including breastplates laden with brasses, floral wreaths and fly head terrets

152 *Right* The village fair at Acle, Norfolk about 1870. The name on the side of the van is Great Eastern Steam Circus

153 *Right, below* The summer fair at Newlyn, near Penzance, Cornwall in 1886 with the Tolcarne watermill in the background

154　The end of the Edwardian era.
Tea at the coronation fête for King
George V held in Came Park,
Winterborne Came, Dorset on 27
June 1911. Everyone is alert for the
photograph except the old man seated
on the left, who appears to be
completely bowed down with his
years